I Can Read, Too

Book 4

Library of Congress Cataloging-in-Publication Data

Sargent, Dave, 1941-
    I can read, too. Book 4 / by Dave and Pat Sargent ; illustrated by Laura Robinson. — Prairie Grove, AR : Ozark Publishing, c2001.
    [24] p. : col. ill. ; 18 x 21 cm. (Learn to read series ; bk. 4)

    SUMMARY: Tells what a variety of animals can do or like, such as an armadillo can dig holes, a cow can moo, a porcupine can climb, and a pig likes mud.
    ISBN: 1-56763-629-2 (hc)
          1-56763-630-6 (pbk)

    [1. Animals—Fiction.] I. Sargent, Pat, 1936- II. Robinson, Laura, 1973- ill.
III. Title. IV. Series.

PZ7. S2465Icd 2001
    [E]—dc21   00-012635

Copyright © 2001 by Dave and Pat Sargent
All rights reserved

Printed in the United States of America

I Can Read, Too

Book 4

by Dave and Pat Sargent

Illustrated by Laura Robinson

Ozark Publishing, Inc.
P.O. Box 228
Prairie Grove, AR 72753

Dave and Pat Sargent, authors of the extremely popular Animal Pride Series, plus many other books, visit schools all over the United States, free of charge.

If you would like to have Dave and Pat visit your school, please ask your librarian to call 1-800-321-5671.

On the last page is a list of vocabulary words and the number of times each word is used.

black fish	fly	porcupine
armadillo	cow	calf
mule	pig	moose

1

I am a black fish.

I can dive.

3

I am a fly.

I can fly.

5

I am a porcupine.

I can climb.

I am an armadillo.

I can dig holes.

I am a cow.

I can moo.

I am a calf.

I like milk.

I am a mule.

I am stubborn.

I am a pig.

I like mud.

I am a moose.

I like to travel.

Below is a list of 25 vocabulary words and the number of times each word is used.

a	6	like	3
am	10	milk	2
an	1	moo	1
armadillo	1	moose	1
blackfish	1	mud	1
calf	1	mule	1
can	5	pig	1
climb	1	porcupine	1
cow	1	stubborn	1
dig	1	to	1
dive	1	travel	1
fly	2		
holes	1		
I	18		

Portage Public Library

31814 88050132 2

Sargent, Dave
I can read, too. Book 4

ER S ES

DATE DUE

E S 8/2004

Sargent, Dave
I can read, too
Book 4

Portage Public Library